STOCK MARKET

This Journal Belongs To

....

Date:	Market Conditions:								
Available Funds:				Stocks ○	Options ○	Futures ○	Forex ○		

Time	Buy/ Sell	Quantity	Name/Symbol	Price	Cost	Proceeds	Net Gain (Loss)	%

Target / Stop	R.O.I. / R.O.R. / R.O.C.

Notes

Investment Plan

Financial Goals	5 Year Target		
	Annual Target		
	Quarterly Target		
Monthly Target	In %	In $	In Pips
Seed Capital	$	Deposit Date	
Replenishment Of The Deposit	$	Deposit Date	
Bonus Funds From A Broker And Size OF Trade/Numbers Of Lots To Get A Bonus	$	Number Of Lots	
	$	Number Of Lots	
The Term To Work Out The Necessary Size Of Trades/Number Of Lots To Get A Bonus	Date		
	Date		
Profit Withdrawal Schedule (% Of Profit And $)	Quarterly/Date	%	$
	Half-Yearly/Date		
	Yearly/Date		

Why I Love Trading

Investment Plan

Notes

Trading Rules

Rules To Open Trade	1	
	2	
	3	
Rules To Close Trade	1	
	2	
	3	
Criteria For A Stop Loss		
Criteria For A Take Profit		
Trade On Time Frames		
Minimum SL To TP Ratio		
Max Trade Size		
Type Of Analysis Used	☐ Technical ☐ Fundamental ☐ Technical + Fundamental	
Rules To Move The Stop Loss Into The Breakeven		
Actions On Trades Left Overnight		
Additional Rules (Trailing, Stop, Averaging, lock, Etc.)	1	
	2	
	3	
	4	

Trading Rules

Notes

Date:	Market Conditions:								
Available Funds:					Stocks ○	Options ○	Futures ○	Forex ○	

Time	Buy/ Sell	Quantity	Name/Symbol	Price	Cost	Proceeds	Net Gain (Loss)	%

Target / Stop	R.O.I. / R.O.R. / R.O.C.

Notes

Date:	Market Conditions:

Available Funds:

	Stocks ○	Options ○	Futures ○	Forex ○

Time	Buy/ Sell	Quantity	Name/Symbol	Price	Cost	Proceeds	Net Gain (Loss)	%

Target / Stop	R.O.I. / R.O.R. / R.O.C.

Notes

Date:	Market Conditions:							

Available Funds:				Stocks ○	Options ○	Futures ○	Forex ○	

Time	Buy/ Sell	Quantity	Name/Symbol	Price	Cost	Proceeds	Net Gain (Loss)	%

Target / Stop	R.O.I. / R.O.R. / R.O.C.

Notes

Date:	Market Conditions:								

Available Funds:

Stocks ○ Options ○ Futures ○ Forex ○

Time	Buy/ Sell	Quantity	Name/Symbol	Price	Cost	Proceeds	Net Gain (Loss)	%

Target / Stop	R.O.I. / R.O.R. / R.O.C.

Notes

Date:	Market Conditions:							

Available Funds:		Stocks ◯	Options ◯	Futures ◯	Forex ◯

Time	Buy/ Sell	Quantity	Name/Symbol	Price	Cost	Proceeds	Net Gain (Loss)	%

Target / Stop	R.O.I. / R.O.R. / R.O.C.

Notes

Date:	Market Conditions:							

Available Funds:				Stocks ○	Options ○	Futures ○	Forex ○	

Time	Buy/ Sell	Quantity	Name/Symbol	Price	Cost	Proceeds	Net Gain (Loss)	%

Target / Stop	R.O.I. / R.O.R. / R.O.C.

Notes

Date:	Market Conditions:						
Available Funds:			Stocks ○	Options ○	Futures ○	Forex ○	

Time	Buy/ Sell	Quantity	Name/Symbol	Price	Cost	Proceeds	Net Gain (Loss)	%

Target / Stop	R.O.I. / R.O.R. / R.O.C.

Notes

Date:	Market Conditions:								

| Available Funds: | | | | Stocks ○ | Options ○ | Futures ○ | Forex ○ | |

Time	Buy/ Sell	Quantity	Name/Symbol	Price	Cost	Proceeds	Net Gain (Loss)	%

Target / Stop	R.O.I. / R.O.R. / R.O.C.

Notes

Date:	Market Conditions:

Available Funds:

Stocks ○   Options ○   Futures ○   Forex ○

Time	Buy/Sell	Quantity	Name/Symbol	Price	Cost	Proceeds	Net Gain (Loss)	%

Target / Stop	R.O.I. / R.O.R. / R.O.C.

Notes

Date:	Market Conditions:							

Available Funds:			Stocks ○	Options ○	Futures ○	Forex ○		

Time	Buy/ Sell	Quantity	Name/Symbol	Price	Cost	Proceeds	Net Gain (Loss)	%

Target / Stop	R.O.I. / R.O.R. / R.O.C.

Notes

Date:	Market Conditions:						

Available Funds:

Stocks ○   Options ○   Futures ○   Forex ○

Time	Buy/ Sell	Quantity	Name/Symbol	Price	Cost	Proceeds	Net Gain (Loss)	%

Target / Stop	R.O.I. / R.O.R. / R.O.C.

Notes

Date:	Market Conditions:								

Available Funds:					Stocks ○	Options ○	Futures ○	Forex ○	

Time	Buy/ Sell	Quantity	Name/Symbol	Price	Cost	Proceeds	Net Gain (Loss)	%

Target / Stop	R.O.I. / R.O.R. / R.O.C.

Notes

Date:	Market Conditions:							

Available Funds:

Stocks ○ Options ○ Futures ○ Forex ○

Time	Buy/Sell	Quantity	Name/Symbol	Price	Cost	Proceeds	Net Gain (Loss)	%

Target / Stop	R.O.I. / R.O.R. / R.O.C.

Notes

Date:	Market Conditions:							

Available Funds:

Stocks ○   Options ○   Futures ○   Forex ○

Time	Buy/ Sell	Quantity	Name/Symbol	Price	Cost	Proceeds	Net Gain (Loss)	%

Target / Stop	R.O.I. / R.O.R. / R.O.C.

Notes

Date:		Market Conditions:						

Available Funds:				Stocks ○	Options ○	Futures ○	Forex ○	

Time	Buy/ Sell	Quantity	Name/Symbol	Price	Cost	Proceeds	Net Gain (Loss)	%

Target / Stop	R.O.I. / R.O.R. / R.O.C.

Notes

Date:		Market Conditions:							

Available Funds:

Stocks ○ Options ○ Futures ○ Forex ○

Time	Buy/ Sell	Quantity	Name/Symbol	Price	Cost	Proceeds	Net Gain (Loss)	%

Target / Stop

R.O.I. / R.O.R. / R.O.C.

Notes

Date:	Market Conditions:							

Available Funds: Stocks ○ Options ○ Futures ○ Forex ○

Time	Buy/ Sell	Quantity	Name/Symbol	Price	Cost	Proceeds	Net Gain (Loss)	%

Target / Stop	R.O.I. / R.O.R. / R.O.C.

Notes

Date:	Market Conditions:								

Available Funds: Stocks ○   Options ○   Futures ○   Forex ○

Time	Buy/ Sell	Quantity	Name/Symbol	Price	Cost	Proceeds	Net Gain (Loss)	%

Target / Stop	R.O.I. / R.O.R. / R.O.C.

Notes

Date:	Market Conditions:							

Available Funds: Stocks ○   Options ○   Futures ○   Forex ○

Time	Buy/Sell	Quantity	Name/Symbol	Price	Cost	Proceeds	Net Gain (Loss)	%

Target / Stop	R.O.I. / R.O.R. / R.O.C.

Notes

Date:	Market Conditions:								

Available Funds: Stocks ○ Options ○ Futures ○ Forex ○

Time	Buy/ Sell	Quantity	Name/Symbol	Price	Cost	Proceeds	Net Gain (Loss)	%

Target / Stop	R.O.I. / R.O.R. / R.O.C.

Notes

Date:	Market Conditions:							

Available Funds:			Stocks ○	Options ○	Futures ○	Forex ○		

Time	Buy/ Sell	Quantity	Name/Symbol	Price	Cost	Proceeds	Net Gain (Loss)	%

Target / Stop	R.O.I. / R.O.R. / R.O.C.

Notes

Date:	Market Conditions:							

Available Funds:			Stocks ○	Options ○	Futures ○	Forex ○

Time	Buy/ Sell	Quantity	Name/Symbol	Price	Cost	Proceeds	Net Gain (Loss)	%

Target / Stop	R.O.I. / R.O.R. / R.O.C.

Notes

Date:	Market Conditions:							

Available Funds:				Stocks ○	Options ○	Futures ○	Forex ○	

Time	Buy/ Sell	Quantity	Name/Symbol	Price	Cost	Proceeds	Net Gain (Loss)	%

Target / Stop	R.O.I. / R.O.R. / R.O.C.

Notes

Date:	Market Conditions:							

Available Funds:

Stocks ○ Options ○ Futures ○ Forex ○

Time	Buy/ Sell	Quantity	Name/Symbol	Price	Cost	Proceeds	Net Gain (Loss)	%

Target / Stop	R.O.I. / R.O.R. / R.O.C.

Notes

Date:	Market Conditions:							

Available Funds:				Stocks ○	Options ○	Futures ○	Forex ○	

Time	Buy/ Sell	Quantity	Name/Symbol	Price	Cost	Proceeds	Net Gain (Loss)	%

Target / Stop	R.O.I. / R.O.R. / R.O.C.

Notes

Date:	Market Conditions:							

Available Funds: Stocks ○   Options ○   Futures ○   Forex ○

Time	Buy/Sell	Quantity	Name/Symbol	Price	Cost	Proceeds	Net Gain (Loss)	%

Target / Stop	R.O.I. / R.O.R. / R.O.C.

Notes

Date:	Market Conditions:							

Available Funds:		Stocks ○	Options ○	Futures ○	Forex ○

Time	Buy/ Sell	Quantity	Name/Symbol	Price	Cost	Proceeds	Net Gain (Loss)	%

Target / Stop	R.O.I. / R.O.R. / R.O.C.

Notes

Date:	Market Conditions:								

Available Funds: Stocks ○   Options ○   Futures ○   Forex ○

Time	Buy/ Sell	Quantity	Name/Symbol	Price	Cost	Proceeds	Net Gain (Loss)	%

Target / Stop	R.O.I. / R.O.R. / R.O.C.

Notes

Date:	Market Conditions:							

Available Funds:				Stocks ○	Options ○	Futures ○	Forex ○	

Time	Buy/ Sell	Quantity	Name/Symbol	Price	Cost	Proceeds	Net Gain (Loss)	%

Target / Stop	R.O.I. / R.O.R. / R.O.C.

Notes

Date:	Market Conditions:							
Available Funds:				Stocks ○	Options ○	Futures ○	Forex ○	

Time	Buy/ Sell	Quantity	Name/Symbol	Price	Cost	Proceeds	Net Gain (Loss)	%

Target / Stop	R.O.I. / R.O.R. / R.O.C.

Notes

Date:	Market Conditions:							

Available Funds:				Stocks ○	Options ○	Futures ○	Forex ○	

Time	Buy/ Sell	Quantity	Name/Symbol	Price	Cost	Proceeds	Net Gain (Loss)	%

Target / Stop	R.O.I. / R.O.R. / R.O.C.

Notes

Date:	Market Conditions:							

Available Funds:

Stocks ○   Options ○   Futures ○   Forex ○

Time	Buy/ Sell	Quantity	Name/Symbol	Price	Cost	Proceeds	Net Gain (Loss)	%

Target / Stop	R.O.I. / R.O.R. / R.O.C.

Notes

Date:	Market Conditions:							

Available Funds:			Stocks ○	Options ○	Futures ○	Forex ○		

Time	Buy/ Sell	Quantity	Name/Symbol	Price	Cost	Proceeds	Net Gain (Loss)	%

Target / Stop	R.O.I. / R.O.R. / R.O.C.

Notes

Date:		Market Conditions:							

Available Funds:					Stocks ○	Options ○	Futures ○	Forex ○	

Time	Buy/ Sell	Quantity	Name/Symbol	Price	Cost	Proceeds	Net Gain (Loss)	%

Target / Stop	R.O.I. / R.O.R. / R.O.C.

Notes

Date:		Market Conditions:						

Available Funds:				Stocks ○	Options ○	Futures ○	Forex ○	

Time	Buy/ Sell	Quantity	Name/Symbol	Price	Cost	Proceeds	Net Gain (Loss)	%

Target / Stop	R.O.I. / R.O.R. / R.O.C.

Notes

Date:	Market Conditions:							

Available Funds:

Stocks ○ Options ○ Futures ○ Forex ○

Time	Buy/ Sell	Quantity	Name/Symbol	Price	Cost	Proceeds	Net Gain (Loss)	%

Target / Stop	R.O.I. / R.O.R. / R.O.C.

Notes

Date:	Market Conditions:							

Available Funds:				Stocks ○	Options ○	Futures ○	Forex ○	

Time	Buy/ Sell	Quantity	Name/Symbol	Price	Cost	Proceeds	Net Gain (Loss)	%

Target / Stop	R.O.I. / R.O.R. / R.O.C.

Notes

Date:	Market Conditions:							

Available Funds:　　　　　　Stocks ○　Options ○　Futures ○　Forex ○

Time	Buy/ Sell	Quantity	Name/Symbol	Price	Cost	Proceeds	Net Gain (Loss)	%

Target / Stop	R.O.I. / R.O.R. / R.O.C.

Notes

Date:	Market Conditions:							

Available Funds: Stocks ○   Options ○   Futures ○   Forex ○

Time	Buy/ Sell	Quantity	Name/Symbol	Price	Cost	Proceeds	Net Gain (Loss)	%

Target / Stop	R.O.I. / R.O.R. / R.O.C.

Notes

Date:	Market Conditions:							

Available Funds:

Stocks ○ Options ○ Futures ○ Forex ○

Time	Buy/Sell	Quantity	Name/Symbol	Price	Cost	Proceeds	Net Gain (Loss)	%

Target / Stop	R.O.I. / R.O.R. / R.O.C.

Notes

Date:	Market Conditions:

Available Funds:		Stocks ○	Options ○	Futures ○	Forex ○

Time	Buy/ Sell	Quantity	Name/Symbol	Price	Cost	Proceeds	Net Gain (Loss)	%

Target / Stop	R.O.I. / R.O.R. / R.O.C.

Notes

Date:		Market Conditions:						

Available Funds:		Stocks ○	Options ○	Futures ○	Forex ○

Time	Buy/ Sell	Quantity	Name/Symbol	Price	Cost	Proceeds	Net Gain (Loss)	%

Target / Stop	R.O.I. / R.O.R. / R.O.C.

Notes

Date:	Market Conditions:				

Available Funds:

Stocks ○ Options ○ Futures ○ Forex ○

Time	Buy/ Sell	Quantity	Name/Symbol	Price	Cost	Proceeds	Net Gain (Loss)	%

Target / Stop	R.O.I. / R.O.R. / R.O.C.

Notes

Date:	Market Conditions:							

Available Funds: Stocks ○ Options ○ Futures ○ Forex ○

Time	Buy/ Sell	Quantity	Name/Symbol	Price	Cost	Proceeds	Net Gain (Loss)	%

Target / Stop	R.O.I. / R.O.R. / R.O.C.

Notes

Date:	Market Conditions:							

Available Funds:				Stocks ○	Options ○	Futures ○	Forex ○	

Time	Buy/ Sell	Quantity	Name/Symbol	Price	Cost	Proceeds	Net Gain (Loss)	%

Target / Stop	R.O.I. / R.O.R. / R.O.C.

Notes

Date:	Market Conditions:

Available Funds:	Stocks ○	Options ○	Futures ○	Forex ○

Time	Buy/ Sell	Quantity	Name/Symbol	Price	Cost	Proceeds	Net Gain (Loss)	%

Target / Stop	R.O.I. / R.O.R. / R.O.C.

Notes

Date:	Market Conditions:								

Available Funds:

Stocks ○ Options ○ Futures ○ Forex ○

Time	Buy/Sell	Quantity	Name/Symbol	Price	Cost	Proceeds	Net Gain (Loss)	%

Target / Stop	R.O.I. / R.O.R. / R.O.C.

Notes

Date:	Market Conditions:							

Available Funds:			Stocks ○	Options ○	Futures ○	Forex ○		

Time	Buy/ Sell	Quantity	Name/Symbol	Price	Cost	Proceeds	Net Gain (Loss)	%

Target / Stop	R.O.I. / R.O.R. / R.O.C.

Notes

Date:		Market Conditions:							
Available Funds:					Stocks ◯	Options ◯	Futures ◯	Forex ◯	

Time	Buy/ Sell	Quantity	Name/Symbol	Price	Cost	Proceeds	Net Gain (Loss)	%

Target / Stop	R.O.I. / R.O.R. / R.O.C.

Notes

Date:	Market Conditions:							

Available Funds: Stocks ○   Options ○   Futures ○   Forex ○

Time	Buy/ Sell	Quantity	Name/Symbol	Price	Cost	Proceeds	Net Gain (Loss)	%

Target / Stop	R.O.I. / R.O.R. / R.O.C.

Notes

| Date: | Market Conditions: | | | | | | | | |

| Available Funds: | | | | | Stocks ○ | Options ○ | Futures ○ | Forex ○ | |

Time	Buy/Sell	Quantity	Name/Symbol	Price	Cost	Proceeds	Net Gain (Loss)	%

| Target / Stop | R.O.I. / R.O.R. / R.O.C. |

Notes

Date:	Market Conditions:							

Available Funds:				Stocks ○	Options ○	Futures ○	Forex ○	

Time	Buy/ Sell	Quantity	Name/Symbol	Price	Cost	Proceeds	Net Gain (Loss)	%

Target / Stop	R.O.I. / R.O.R. / R.O.C.

Notes

Date:	Market Conditions:							

Available Funds:				Stocks ○	Options ○	Futures ○	Forex ○	

Time	Buy/ Sell	Quantity	Name/Symbol	Price	Cost	Proceeds	Net Gain (Loss)	%

Target / Stop				R.O.I. / R.O.R. / R.O.C.				

Notes

Date:	Market Conditions:						

Available Funds:

Stocks ○   Options ○   Futures ○   Forex ○

Time	Buy/ Sell	Quantity	Name/Symbol	Price	Cost	Proceeds	Net Gain (Loss)	%

Target / Stop	R.O.I. / R.O.R. / R.O.C.

Notes

Date:	Market Conditions:							

Available Funds: Stocks ○ Options ○ Futures ○ Forex ○

Time	Buy/Sell	Quantity	Name/Symbol	Price	Cost	Proceeds	Net Gain (Loss)	%

Target / Stop	R.O.I. / R.O.R. / R.O.C.

Notes

Date:	Market Conditions:								

Available Funds:

Stocks ○ Options ○ Futures ○ Forex ○

Time	Buy/ Sell	Quantity	Name/Symbol	Price	Cost	Proceeds	Net Gain (Loss)	%

Target / Stop	R.O.I. / R.O.R. / R.O.C.

Notes

| Date: | Market Conditions: | | | | | | | |

Available Funds: Stocks ○   Options ○   Futures ○   Forex ○

Time	Buy/ Sell	Quantity	Name/Symbol	Price	Cost	Proceeds	Net Gain (Loss)	%

Target / Stop	R.O.I. / R.O.R. / R.O.C.

Notes

Date:	Market Conditions:								

Available Funds: Stocks ◯   Options ◯   Futures ◯   Forex ◯

Time	Buy/Sell	Quantity	Name/Symbol	Price	Cost	Proceeds	Net Gain (Loss)	%

Target / Stop	R.O.I. / R.O.R. / R.O.C.

Notes

Date:		Market Conditions:							

Available Funds:				Stocks ○	Options ○	Futures ○	Forex ○		

Time	Buy/ Sell	Quantity	Name/Symbol	Price	Cost	Proceeds	Net Gain (Loss)	%

Target / Stop	R.O.I. / R.O.R. / R.O.C.

Notes

Date:	Market Conditions:							

Available Funds:			Stocks ◯	Options ◯	Futures ◯	Forex ◯

Time	Buy/ Sell	Quantity	Name/Symbol	Price	Cost	Proceeds	Net Gain (Loss)	%

Target / Stop	R.O.I. / R.O.R. / R.O.C.

Notes

Date:	Market Conditions:

Available Funds:

Stocks ○ Options ○ Futures ○ Forex ○

Time	Buy/ Sell	Quantity	Name/Symbol	Price	Cost	Proceeds	Net Gain (Loss)	%

Target / Stop	R.O.I. / R.O.R. / R.O.C.

Notes

Date:	Market Conditions:							

Available Funds:

Stocks ○   Options ○   Futures ○   Forex ○

Time	Buy/ Sell	Quantity	Name/Symbol	Price	Cost	Proceeds	Net Gain (Loss)	%

Target / Stop	R.O.I. / R.O.R. / R.O.C.

Notes

Date:	Market Conditions:							

Available Funds:		Stocks ○	Options ○	Futures ○	Forex ○

Time	Buy/ Sell	Quantity	Name/Symbol	Price	Cost	Proceeds	Net Gain (Loss)	%

Target / Stop	R.O.I. / R.O.R. / R.O.C.

Notes

Date:	Market Conditions:								

Available Funds:				Stocks ○	Options ○	Futures ○	Forex ○		

Time	Buy/ Sell	Quantity	Name/Symbol	Price	Cost	Proceeds	Net Gain (Loss)	%

Target / Stop	R.O.I. / R.O.R. / R.O.C.

Notes

Date:	Market Conditions:

Available Funds:

Stocks ○	Options ○	Futures ○	Forex ○

Time	Buy/Sell	Quantity	Name/Symbol	Price	Cost	Proceeds	Net Gain (Loss)	%

Target / Stop	R.O.I. / R.O.R. / R.O.C.

Notes

Date:	Market Conditions:							

Available Funds: Stocks ◯ Options ◯ Futures ◯ Forex ◯

Time	Buy/ Sell	Quantity	Name/Symbol	Price	Cost	Proceeds	Net Gain (Loss)	%

Target / Stop	R.O.I. / R.O.R. / R.O.C.

Notes

Date:	Market Conditions:

Available Funds:

Stocks ○ Options ○ Futures ○ Forex ○

Time	Buy/ Sell	Quantity	Name/Symbol	Price	Cost	Proceeds	Net Gain (Loss)	%

Target / Stop	R.O.I. / R.O.R. / R.O.C.

Notes

Date:	Market Conditions:							

Available Funds:

Stocks ◯ Options ◯ Futures ◯ Forex ◯

Time	Buy/ Sell	Quantity	Name/Symbol	Price	Cost	Proceeds	Net Gain (Loss)	%

Target / Stop	R.O.I. / R.O.R. / R.O.C.

Notes

Date:	Market Conditions:

Available Funds:	Stocks ○	Options ○	Futures ○	Forex ○

Time	Buy/ Sell	Quantity	Name/Symbol	Price	Cost	Proceeds	Net Gain (Loss)	%

Target / Stop	R.O.I. / R.O.R. / R.O.C.

Notes

Date:	Market Conditions:							

Available Funds:				Stocks ○	Options ○	Futures ○	Forex ○	

Time	Buy/ Sell	Quantity	Name/Symbol	Price	Cost	Proceeds	Net Gain (Loss)	%

Target / Stop	R.O.I. / R.O.R. / R.O.C.

Notes

Date:	Market Conditions:								

Available Funds:

Stocks ○ Options ○ Futures ○ Forex ○

Time	Buy/Sell	Quantity	Name/Symbol	Price	Cost	Proceeds	Net Gain (Loss)	%

Target / Stop	R.O.I. / R.O.R. / R.O.C.

Notes

Date:	Market Conditions:						

Available Funds:

Stocks ○   Options ○   Futures ○   Forex ○

Time	Buy/ Sell	Quantity	Name/Symbol	Price	Cost	Proceeds	Net Gain (Loss)	%

Target / Stop	R.O.I. / R.O.R. / R.O.C.

Notes

| Date: | Market Conditions: | | | | | | | |

Available Funds:

| Stocks ◯ | Options ◯ | Futures ◯ | Forex ◯ |

Time	Buy/Sell	Quantity	Name/Symbol	Price	Cost	Proceeds	Net Gain (Loss)	%

| Target / Stop | R.O.I. / R.O.R. / R.O.C. |

Notes

Date:	Market Conditions:							

Available Funds:				Stocks ○	Options ○	Futures ○	Forex ○	

Time	Buy/ Sell	Quantity	Name/Symbol	Price	Cost	Proceeds	Net Gain (Loss)	%

Target / Stop	R.O.I. / R.O.R. / R.O.C.

Notes

Date:	Market Conditions:							

Available Funds:				Stocks ○	Options ○	Futures ○	Forex ○	

Time	Buy/ Sell	Quantity	Name/Symbol	Price	Cost	Proceeds	Net Gain (Loss)	%

Target / Stop	R.O.I. / R.O.R. / R.O.C.

Notes

Date:	Market Conditions:							

Available Funds:

Stocks ○ Options ○ Futures ○ Forex ○

Time	Buy/ Sell	Quantity	Name/Symbol	Price	Cost	Proceeds	Net Gain (Loss)	%

Target / Stop	R.O.I. / R.O.R. / R.O.C.

Notes

Date:	Market Conditions:						

Available Funds:

Stocks ○ Options ○ Futures ○ Forex ○

Time	Buy/ Sell	Quantity	Name/Symbol	Price	Cost	Proceeds	Net Gain (Loss)	%

Target / Stop	R.O.I. / R.O.R. / R.O.C.

Notes

Date:	Market Conditions:

Available Funds:

Stocks ○	Options ○	Futures ○	Forex ○

Time	Buy/ Sell	Quantity	Name/Symbol	Price	Cost	Proceeds	Net Gain (Loss)	%

Target / Stop	R.O.I. / R.O.R. / R.O.C.

Notes

Date:	Market Conditions:							

Available Funds:

Stocks ○ Options ○ Futures ○ Forex ○

Time	Buy/ Sell	Quantity	Name/Symbol	Price	Cost	Proceeds	Net Gain (Loss)	%

Target / Stop	R.O.I. / R.O.R. / R.O.C.

Notes

Date:	Market Conditions:							

Available Funds:　　　　Stocks ○　Options ○　Futures ○　Forex ○

Time	Buy/ Sell	Quantity	Name/Symbol	Price	Cost	Proceeds	Net Gain (Loss)	%

Target / Stop	R.O.I. / R.O.R. / R.O.C.

Notes

Date:	Market Conditions:								

Available Funds:

Stocks ○   Options ○   Futures ○   Forex ○

Time	Buy/ Sell	Quantity	Name/Symbol	Price	Cost	Proceeds	Net Gain (Loss)	%

Target / Stop	R.O.I. / R.O.R. / R.O.C.

Notes

Date:	Market Conditions:							

Available Funds:					Stocks ◯	Options ◯	Futures ◯	Forex ◯

Time	Buy/ Sell	Quantity	Name/Symbol	Price	Cost	Proceeds	Net Gain (Loss)	%

Target / Stop	R.O.I. / R.O.R. / R.O.C.

Notes

Date:	Market Conditions:							

Available Funds:

Stocks ○ Options ○ Futures ○ Forex ○

Time	Buy/ Sell	Quantity	Name/Symbol	Price	Cost	Proceeds	Net Gain (Loss)	%

Target / Stop	R.O.I. / R.O.R. / R.O.C.

Notes

Date:	Market Conditions:

Available Funds:

Stocks ○ Options ○ Futures ○ Forex ○

Time	Buy/ Sell	Quantity	Name/Symbol	Price	Cost	Proceeds	Net Gain (Loss)	%

Target / Stop	R.O.I. / R.O.R. / R.O.C.

Notes

Date:	Market Conditions:								

Available Funds: Stocks ○   Options ○   Futures ○   Forex ○

Time	Buy/ Sell	Quantity	Name/Symbol	Price	Cost	Proceeds	Net Gain (Loss)	%

Target / Stop	R.O.I. / R.O.R. / R.O.C.

Notes

Date:	Market Conditions:							

Available Funds:

Stocks ○ Options ○ Futures ○ Forex ○

Time	Buy/ Sell	Quantity	Name/Symbol	Price	Cost	Proceeds	Net Gain (Loss)	%

Target / Stop	R.O.I. / R.O.R. / R.O.C.

Notes

Date:	Market Conditions:							

Available Funds: Stocks ○ Options ○ Futures ○ Forex ○

Time	Buy/ Sell	Quantity	Name/Symbol	Price	Cost	Proceeds	Net Gain (Loss)	%

Target / Stop	R.O.I. / R.O.R. / R.O.C.

Notes

Date:	Market Conditions:							

Available Funds:

Stocks ○   Options ○   Futures ○   Forex ○

Time	Buy/Sell	Quantity	Name/Symbol	Price	Cost	Proceeds	Net Gain (Loss)	%

Target / Stop   R.O.I. / R.O.R. / R.O.C.

Notes

Date:	Market Conditions:							

Available Funds:		Stocks ○	Options ○	Futures ○	Forex ○

Time	Buy/ Sell	Quantity	Name/Symbol	Price	Cost	Proceeds	Net Gain (Loss)	%

Target / Stop	R.O.I. / R.O.R. / R.O.C.

Notes

Date:	Market Conditions:							

Available Funds:					Stocks ○	Options ○	Futures ○	Forex ○

Time	Buy/ Sell	Quantity	Name/Symbol	Price	Cost	Proceeds	Net Gain (Loss)	%

Target / Stop	R.O.I. / R.O.R. / R.O.C.

Notes

Date:	Market Conditions:							

Available Funds: Stocks ○   Options ○   Futures ○   Forex ○

Time	Buy/ Sell	Quantity	Name/Symbol	Price	Cost	Proceeds	Net Gain (Loss)	%

Target / Stop	R.O.I. / R.O.R. / R.O.C.

Notes

Date:	Market Conditions:								

Available Funds: Stocks ◯   Options ◯   Futures ◯   Forex ◯

Time	Buy/ Sell	Quantity	Name/Symbol	Price	Cost	Proceeds	Net Gain (Loss)	%

Target / Stop	R.O.I. / R.O.R. / R.O.C.

Notes

Date:		Market Conditions:							

Available Funds: Stocks ○ Options ○ Futures ○ Forex ○

Time	Buy/ Sell	Quantity	Name/Symbol	Price	Cost	Proceeds	Net Gain (Loss)	%

Target / Stop	R.O.I. / R.O.R. / R.O.C.

Notes

Date:	Market Conditions:

Available Funds:

Stocks ○ Options ○ Futures ○ Forex ○

Time	Buy/ Sell	Quantity	Name/Symbol	Price	Cost	Proceeds	Net Gain (Loss)	%

Target / Stop	R.O.I. / R.O.R. / R.O.C.

Notes

Date:	Market Conditions:							

Available Funds: Stocks ○   Options ○   Futures ○   Forex ○

Time	Buy/Sell	Quantity	Name/Symbol	Price	Cost	Proceeds	Net Gain (Loss)	%

Target / Stop	R.O.I. / R.O.R. / R.O.C.

Notes

Date:	Market Conditions:							

Available Funds:

Stocks ○ Options ○ Futures ○ Forex ○

Time	Buy/ Sell	Quantity	Name/Symbol	Price	Cost	Proceeds	Net Gain (Loss)	%

Target / Stop	R.O.I. / R.O.R. / R.O.C.

Notes

Date:		Market Conditions:							

Available Funds:				Stocks ○	Options ○	Futures ○	Forex ○		

Time	Buy/ Sell	Quantity	Name/Symbol	Price	Cost	Proceeds	Net Gain (Loss)	%

Target / Stop	R.O.I. / R.O.R. / R.O.C.

Notes

Date:	Market Conditions:		

Available Funds:

Stocks ○ Options ○ Futures ○ Forex ○

Time	Buy/ Sell	Quantity	Name/Symbol	Price	Cost	Proceeds	Net Gain (Loss)	%

Target / Stop	R.O.I. / R.O.R. / R.O.C.

Notes

Date:	Market Conditions:

Available Funds:

Stocks ○ Options ○ Futures ○ Forex ○

Time	Buy/ Sell	Quantity	Name/Symbol	Price	Cost	Proceeds	Net Gain (Loss)	%

Target / Stop	R.O.I. / R.O.R. / R.O.C.

Notes

Date:	Market Conditions:

Available Funds:

Stocks ○ Options ○ Futures ○ Forex ○

Time	Buy/Sell	Quantity	Name/Symbol	Price	Cost	Proceeds	Net Gain (Loss)	%

Target / Stop	R.O.I. / R.O.R. / R.O.C.

Notes

Date:	Market Conditions:							

Available Funds:				Stocks ○	Options ○	Futures ○	Forex ○	

Time	Buy/ Sell	Quantity	Name/Symbol	Price	Cost	Proceeds	Net Gain (Loss)	%

Target / Stop	R.O.I. / R.O.R. / R.O.C.

Notes

Date:	Market Conditions:								

Available Funds:

Stocks ○ Options ○ Futures ○ Forex ○

Time	Buy/ Sell	Quantity	Name/Symbol	Price	Cost	Proceeds	Net Gain (Loss)	%

Target / Stop	R.O.I. / R.O.R. / R.O.C.

Notes

Date:	Market Conditions:						

Available Funds: Stocks ○   Options ○   Futures ○   Forex ○

Time	Buy/ Sell	Quantity	Name/Symbol	Price	Cost	Proceeds	Net Gain (Loss)	%

Target / Stop	R.O.I. / R.O.R. / R.O.C.

Notes

Date:	Market Conditions:							

Available Funds:				Stocks ○	Options ○	Futures ○	Forex ○	

Time	Buy/Sell	Quantity	Name/Symbol	Price	Cost	Proceeds	Net Gain (Loss)	%

Target / Stop	R.O.I. / R.O.R. / R.O.C.

Notes

Date:	Market Conditions:							

Available Funds:

Stocks ○ Options ○ Futures ○ Forex ○

Time	Buy/Sell	Quantity	Name/Symbol	Price	Cost	Proceeds	Net Gain (Loss)	%

Target / Stop	R.O.I. / R.O.R. / R.O.C.

Notes

Date:	Market Conditions:						

Available Funds:

Stocks ○ Options ○ Futures ○ Forex ○

Time	Buy/ Sell	Quantity	Name/Symbol	Price	Cost	Proceeds	Net Gain (Loss)	%

Target / Stop	R.O.I. / R.O.R. / R.O.C.

Notes

Date:	Market Conditions:						

Available Funds:

Stocks ○   Options ○   Futures ○   Forex ○

Time	Buy/ Sell	Quantity	Name/Symbol	Price	Cost	Proceeds	Net Gain (Loss)	%

Target / Stop	R.O.I. / R.O.R. / R.O.C.

Notes

Date:	Market Conditions:							

Available Funds:

Stocks ○ Options ○ Futures ○ Forex ○

Time	Buy/ Sell	Quantity	Name/Symbol	Price	Cost	Proceeds	Net Gain (Loss)	%

Target / Stop	R.O.I. / R.O.R. / R.O.C.

Notes

Date:	Market Conditions:			

Available Funds:

Stocks ○ Options ○ Futures ○ Forex ○

Time	Buy/ Sell	Quantity	Name/Symbol	Price	Cost	Proceeds	Net Gain (Loss)	%

Target / Stop	R.O.I. / R.O.R. / R.O.C.

Notes

Date:	Market Conditions:							

Available Funds:

Stocks ○ Options ○ Futures ○ Forex ○

Time	Buy/ Sell	Quantity	Name/Symbol	Price	Cost	Proceeds	Net Gain (Loss)	%

Target / Stop

R.O.I. / R.O.R. / R.O.C.

Notes

Date:		Market Conditions:						

Available Funds:

Stocks ○   Options ○   Futures ○   Forex ○

Time	Buy/ Sell	Quantity	Name/Symbol	Price	Cost	Proceeds	Net Gain (Loss)	%

Target / Stop   R.O.I. / R.O.R. / R.O.C.

Notes

Date:	Market Conditions:							

Available Funds:

Stocks ○ Options ○ Futures ○ Forex ○

Time	Buy/ Sell	Quantity	Name/Symbol	Price	Cost	Proceeds	Net Gain (Loss)	%

Target / Stop	R.O.I. / R.O.R. / R.O.C.

Notes

Date:	Market Conditions:							

Available Funds:

Stocks ○ Options ○ Futures ○ Forex ○

Time	Buy/ Sell	Quantity	Name/Symbol	Price	Cost	Proceeds	Net Gain (Loss)	%

Target / Stop	R.O.I. / R.O.R. / R.O.C.

Notes

Date:		Market Conditions:							

Available Funds:			Stocks ○	Options ○	Futures ○	Forex ○

Time	Buy/ Sell	Quantity	Name/Symbol	Price	Cost	Proceeds	Net Gain (Loss)	%

Target / Stop	R.O.I. / R.O.R. / R.O.C.

Notes

Date:		Market Conditions:						

Available Funds:			Stocks ○	Options ○	Futures ○	Forex ○		

Time	Buy/ Sell	Quantity	Name/Symbol	Price	Cost	Proceeds	Net Gain (Loss)	%

Target / Stop	R.O.I. / R.O.R. / R.O.C.

Notes

Date:		Market Conditions:						

Available Funds:				Stocks ○	Options ○	Futures ○	Forex ○	

Time	Buy/ Sell	Quantity	Name/Symbol	Price	Cost	Proceeds	Net Gain (Loss)	%

Target / Stop	R.O.I. / R.O.R. / R.O.C.

Notes

Date:		Market Conditions:							

Available Funds:				Stocks ○	Options ○	Futures ○	Forex ○		

Time	Buy/Sell	Quantity	Name/Symbol	Price	Cost	Proceeds	Net Gain (Loss)	%

Target / Stop	R.O.I. / R.O.R. / R.O.C.

Notes

Date:	Market Conditions:							

Available Funds:			Stocks ○	Options ○	Futures ○	Forex ○		

Time	Buy/ Sell	Quantity	Name/Symbol	Price	Cost	Proceeds	Net Gain (Loss)	%

Target / Stop	R.O.I. / R.O.R. / R.O.C.

Notes

Date:	Market Conditions:								

Available Funds: Stocks ○ Options ○ Futures ○ Forex ○

Time	Buy/ Sell	Quantity	Name/Symbol	Price	Cost	Proceeds	Net Gain (Loss)	%

Target / Stop	R.O.I. / R.O.R. / R.O.C.

Notes

Date:	Market Conditions:								

Available Funds: _____ Stocks ○ Options ○ Futures ○ Forex ○

Time	Buy/ Sell	Quantity	Name/Symbol	Price	Cost	Proceeds	Net Gain (Loss)	%

Target / Stop _____   R.O.I. / R.O.R. / R.O.C. _____

Notes

Date:	Market Conditions:						

Available Funds:

Stocks ○   Options ○   Futures ○   Forex ○

Time	Buy/ Sell	Quantity	Name/Symbol	Price	Cost	Proceeds	Net Gain (Loss)	%

Target / Stop

R.O.I. / R.O.R. / R.O.C.

Notes

Date:	Market Conditions:

Available Funds:

Stocks ○	Options ○	Futures ○	Forex ○

Time	Buy/Sell	Quantity	Name/Symbol	Price	Cost	Proceeds	Net Gain (Loss)	%

Target / Stop	R.O.I. / R.O.R. / R.O.C.

Notes

Date:	Market Conditions:							

Available Funds: Stocks ○   Options ○   Futures ○   Forex ○

Time	Buy/Sell	Quantity	Name/Symbol	Price	Cost	Proceeds	Net Gain (Loss)	%

Target / Stop	R.O.I. / R.O.R. / R.O.C.

Notes

Date:	Market Conditions:								

Available Funds: | Stocks ○ | Options ○ | Futures ○ | Forex ○

Time	Buy/ Sell	Quantity	Name/Symbol	Price	Cost	Proceeds	Net Gain (Loss)	%

Target / Stop | R.O.I. / R.O.R. / R.O.C.

Notes

Date:	Market Conditions:							

Available Funds:

Stocks ○ Options ○ Futures ○ Forex ○

Time	Buy/Sell	Quantity	Name/Symbol	Price	Cost	Proceeds	Net Gain (Loss)	%

Target / Stop	R.O.I. / R.O.R. / R.O.C.

Notes

Date:	Market Conditions:								

Available Funds:				Stocks ○	Options ○	Futures ○	Forex ○		
Time	Buy/ Sell	Quantity	Name/Symbol	Price	Cost	Proceeds	Net Gain (Loss)	%	

Target / Stop	R.O.I. / R.O.R. / R.O.C.

Notes

Date:	Market Conditions:								
Available Funds:				Stocks ○	Options ○	Futures ○	Forex ○		

Time	Buy/ Sell	Quantity	Name/Symbol	Price	Cost	Proceeds	Net Gain (Loss)	%

Target / Stop	R.O.I. / R.O.R. / R.O.C.

Notes

Date:	Market Conditions:							

Available Funds: Stocks ○   Options ○   Futures ○   Forex ○

Time	Buy/ Sell	Quantity	Name/Symbol	Price	Cost	Proceeds	Net Gain (Loss)	%

Target / Stop	R.O.I. / R.O.R. / R.O.C.

Notes

Date:	Market Conditions:							

Available Funds:				Stocks ○	Options ○	Futures ○	Forex ○	

Time	Buy/Sell	Quantity	Name/Symbol	Price	Cost	Proceeds	Net Gain (Loss)	%

Target / Stop	R.O.I. / R.O.R. / R.O.C.

Notes

Date:		Market Conditions:						

Available Funds: Stocks ○   Options ○   Futures ○   Forex ○

Time	Buy/Sell	Quantity	Name/Symbol	Price	Cost	Proceeds	Net Gain (Loss)	%

Target / Stop	R.O.I. / R.O.R. / R.O.C.

Notes

Date:	Market Conditions:							

Available Funds:		Stocks ○	Options ○	Futures ○	Forex ○

Time	Buy/ Sell	Quantity	Name/Symbol	Price	Cost	Proceeds	Net Gain (Loss)	%

Target / Stop	R.O.I. / R.O.R. / R.O.C.

Notes

Date:	Market Conditions:							

Available Funds:

Stocks ○ Options ○ Futures ○ Forex ○

Time	Buy/ Sell	Quantity	Name/Symbol	Price	Cost	Proceeds	Net Gain (Loss)	%

Target / Stop	R.O.I. / R.O.R. / R.O.C.

Notes

Date:	Market Conditions:

Available Funds:

Stocks ○   Options ○   Futures ○   Forex ○

Time	Buy/ Sell	Quantity	Name/Symbol	Price	Cost	Proceeds	Net Gain (Loss)	%

Target / Stop	R.O.I. / R.O.R. / R.O.C.

Notes

Date:	Market Conditions:								

Available Funds:					Stocks ○	Options ○	Futures ○	Forex ○	

Time	Buy/ Sell	Quantity	Name/Symbol	Price	Cost	Proceeds	Net Gain (Loss)	%

Target / Stop	R.O.I. / R.O.R. / R.O.C.

Notes

Date:	Market Conditions:							

Available Funds:

Stocks ○ Options ○ Futures ○ Forex ○

Time	Buy/ Sell	Quantity	Name/Symbol	Price	Cost	Proceeds	Net Gain (Loss)	%

Target / Stop	R.O.I. / R.O.R. / R.O.C.

Notes

Date:	Market Conditions:							

Available Funds: Stocks ○   Options ○   Futures ○   Forex ○

Time	Buy/ Sell	Quantity	Name/Symbol	Price	Cost	Proceeds	Net Gain (Loss)	%

Target / Stop	R.O.I. / R.O.R. / R.O.C.

Notes

Date:		Market Conditions:						

Available Funds:				Stocks ○	Options ○	Futures ○	Forex ○

Time	Buy/ Sell	Quantity	Name/Symbol	Price	Cost	Proceeds	Net Gain (Loss)	%

Target / Stop	R.O.I. / R.O.R. / R.O.C.

Notes

Date:	Market Conditions:							

Available Funds:

Stocks ○   Options ○   Futures ○   Forex ○

Time	Buy/Sell	Quantity	Name/Symbol	Price	Cost	Proceeds	Net Gain (Loss)	%

Target / Stop	R.O.I. / R.O.R. / R.O.C.

Notes

Date:	Market Conditions:									
Available Funds:				Stocks ○	Options ○	Futures ○	Forex ○			

Time	Buy/ Sell	Quantity	Name/Symbol	Price	Cost	Proceeds	Net Gain (Loss)	%

Target / Stop	R.O.I. / R.O.R. / R.O.C.

Notes

Date:	Market Conditions:							

Available Funds:

Stocks ○ Options ○ Futures ○ Forex ○

Time	Buy/ Sell	Quantity	Name/Symbol	Price	Cost	Proceeds	Net Gain (Loss)	%

Target / Stop	R.O.I. / R.O.R. / R.O.C.

Notes

Date:	Market Conditions:							

Available Funds:			Stocks ○	Options ○	Futures ○	Forex ○		

Time	Buy/ Sell	Quantity	Name/Symbol	Price	Cost	Proceeds	Net Gain (Loss)	%

Target / Stop	R.O.I. / R.O.R. / R.O.C.

Notes

| Date: | Market Conditions: | | | | | | | | |

| Available Funds: | | | | Stocks ○ | Options ○ | Futures ○ | Forex ○ | | |

Time	Buy/ Sell	Quantity	Name/Symbol	Price	Cost	Proceeds	Net Gain (Loss)	%

| Target / Stop | R.O.I. / R.O.R. / R.O.C. |

Notes

Date:	Market Conditions:							

Available Funds:				Stocks ○	Options ○	Futures ○	Forex ○	

Time	Buy/ Sell	Quantity	Name/Symbol	Price	Cost	Proceeds	Net Gain (Loss)	%

Target / Stop	R.O.I. / R.O.R. / R.O.C.

Notes

Thankyou
You Are Awesome

Dear Trader

Producing this book was a one-man operation, and it took a lot of hard work to bring this quality content to you guys. I don't have a huge budget like other big publishers for advertising .

If you like this book , please spend a moment to add a review on amazon.com. This will help others to find the book.

Each and everyone of your reviews is paramount to me and for my survival as it helps me to compete against larger corporations.

I am **forever** grateful for your support .